AMI HARTS

DESIGN YOUR FUTURE

The Ultimate Guide on Getting Everything You Want in Life, Learn Useful Strategies on Training Your Brain to Realize Your Goals and Get What You Really Want

Descrierea CIP a Bibliotecii Naţionale a României
AMI HARTS
    DESIGN YOUR FUTURE. The Ultimate Guide on Getting
Everything You Want in Life, Learn Useful Strategies on
Training Your Brain to Realize Your Goals and Get What You
Really Want / Ami Harts. – Bucharest: Editura My Ebook, 2020
    ISBN 978-606-983-581-4

AMI HARTS

DESIGN YOUR FUTURE

The Ultimate Guide on Getting Everything You Want in Life, Learn Useful Strategies on Training Your Brain to Realize Your Goals and Get What You Really Want

My Ebook Publishing House
Bucharest, 2020

CONTENTS

Introduction   7

Chapter 1. **What Do You Really Want ?**   9

Chapter 2. **Setting Goals, The Right Way**   17

Chapter 3. **Plan To Get What You Want**   23

Chapter 4. **Control Your Thoughts To Get What You Want**   33

Chapter 5. **Developing The Mental Toughness To Get What You Want**   45

Chapter 6. **Using The Law Of Attraction To Get What You Want**   55

Chapter 7. **Raise Your Confidence Levels To GetWhat You Really Want**   61

Chapter 8. **Your Daily Routine For Getting What You Really Want**   65

Chapter 9. **Best Practices For Getting What You Really Want** …………………………………….. 69

Conclusion ……………………………………………… 75

Introduction

You can get what you really want in your life if you know how to go about it in the right way. This guide will show you exactly how to do that. Most people have no idea what they really want in their life and as a result they let life control them and end up being bitterly disappointed.

The first thing that you need to accept is that getting what you want is going to take time and effort. The reason that most people don't know what they really want is that they cannot be bothered to think about it deeply. They would sooner waste their time on social media or watching nonsense on TV.

The first step to get what you really want is to decide what you really want. To do this you will need to spend some quality time away from any distractions and ask yourself a number of searching questions. There are many examples of these questions in the first chapter of this guide.

Then you need to set your goals properly and create a plan for achieving your goals. When you create plans they will never be perfect so accept that you will need to review them regularly and make the necessary adjustments to them.

The most critical aspect of getting what you really want is controlling your thoughts. If you don't deal with the negative thoughts that we all experience properly then you will never manifest your desires. You also need to develop a mental toughness to deal with setbacks and keep you on the right track.

Everything that you need to know about getting what you really want is in this powerful guide. So read every word and apply what you learn. The steps outlined in the guide require practice, patience and persistence.

What Do You Really Want?

Chapter 1

The reason why most people do not get what they really want in their lives is because they don't know what they want. If you were go to a busy shopping mall on any weekend and ask a number of randomly selected people what they really want from their life then you are likely to get a lot of "I don't know" or "I haven't really thought about it" type answers.

So why is this?

Well there are a couple of reasons. The first is that thinking about what you really want from life requires effort and most people would prefer to waste time watching TV or sitting on social media for hours.

The second reason is that as we progress through life it is easy to think that you already have what you want. You have a steady job with steady income, a life partner, wonderful children, your own home, two cars and so on. What else could you possibly want?

Dare to Dream

These days we are surrounded by motivational messages telling us to go after what we really want. So why do so many people fail to do this? Most people do not have a clue what they want but there are always exceptions of course.

There are people that dream of becoming successful in business, politics, sport, music, art, the movies etc. These people dare to dream. But the sad fact is that most of these "dreamers" will never achieve what they really want.

Why is this?

Well they do not have the mindset to do it. They have big dreams but that's all they are – dreams. These people do not possess the right mentality to follow through and make it happen. And that is what this guide is all about. Providing you with the tools and techniques to change your mindset so that you will have every chance of getting what you really want.

But it all starts by knowing what you really want. Having the right success mindset will do nothing for you if you do not have clarity over what it is you truly desire. So in this chapter we are going to help you to determine what you really want.

How to Discover what you really want

This is going to require you to take some quality time out without distractions. Put your phone on silent and go into a room that does not have a computer or TV. Tell other members of your household that you don't want to be disturbed unless there is an emergency. Arm yourself with a pen and a few sheets of paper and you are ready to go.

What you are going to do now is to take a look at different areas of your life. We are going to provide you with some questions to ask yourself in the following areas:

- Your Job or Business

- Your Finances

- Your Personal Life

- Your Health and Wellbeing

- Your Contribution

This is by no means an exhaustive list. Once you have been through these life areas you can add others if you wish. But these will give you a great start in determining what you really want. With each of these questions you need to write an answer down on paper. Don't worry about how you are going to achieve these things – we will tackle this later.

So here we go…

Your Job or Business

- Are you earning enough money?

- Are you happy in your job or running your business?

- Do you need to improve specific business skills e.g. leadership skills, public speaking skills, writing skills?

- Do you want a promotion in your job?

- Do you want to start a home business?

- Do you need to take care of your customers better?

- Are you happy with your company's career path?

- Do you want to have a different role at work or move to another department?

- Do you need to learn more about your industry?

- Do you like the industry you are in?

Your Finances

- Do you have money growing in a savings account?

- Does your savings account provide you with the highest rate of interest?

- Do you have any debts?

- Do you want to make investments?

- Do you have a pension plan?

- Do you have life insurance for you and your family?

- Do you have complete control over your finances?

- Are you happy with your bank?

- Do you want to learn how the financial markets work?

- Are your taxes in order?

Your Personal Life

Do you have high self esteem? Do you like where you live?

If you rent do you want to buy your own home? Do you take care of your home?

Do you want a bigger home?

Do you have a partner in your life? Do you want to find love?

Do you have a supportive circle of friends? Do you want new clothes?

Do you want to start a new hobby? Do you want to learn a new skill?

Your Health and Wellbeing

- Are you in good health?

- Do you need to lose some weight?

- Do you need to gain some weight?

- Do you exercise regularly?

- Do you want cosmetic surgery?

- Do you require more self confidence?

- Do you truly love yourself?

Your Contribution

- Do you do enough to help others?

- Do you contribute to worthy causes?

- Do you have good relationships with others?

- Do you want to do community work?

- Do you help your family and friends enough?

- Do you listen to others?

OK now you need to take a look at what you have written on your paper. What are some of the things that you wrote down? Do you want more money? Do you want a partner to love? Do you want to give more?

For each of the things that you listed think about how having these things in your life will make you feel. Write down the feelings that you experience. This is not difficult to do but it is vital in determining what you really want. You need to prioritize your list so the things that provoke the strongest feelings within you are at the top.

If you do not have particularly strong feelings about any of the things that you wrote down then go through the exercise again and use different questions. It is critical that you find those things which really stir your emotions so that you can move forward.

Now that you have your shortlist of things that you really want it is a good idea to look at them again and choose a maximum of 3. This is because each one is likely to require some significant effort and a real change in your thinking to achieve them.

So for example if one of the things that you really want is to start your own business and earn a significant income then you can do this at the same time as losing weight and exercising. If you take on too many things then you are unlikely to succeed with any of them.

In the next chapter we will be showing you how to turn these things that you really want into goals that you will strive to achieve…

Setting Goals, The Right Way

Chapter 2

Congratulate yourself because you now know what you really want which puts you in an elite group which represents only 1 – 3% of the population. You should feel really excited now because you finally have clarity. Clarity is power and now we are going to take this a step further by turning the things that you want into actionable goals.

Just having a list of goals is not much use. OK it is better than not having any goals at all but that's about it. How many times did you set yourself New Year's resolutions and failed by the third day in January? It's OK because the vast majority of people do this.

The main reason is that people say things like "I will lose weight next year" or "I will earn more money next year". The trouble is with these statements is that they are not specific. If you lose half a pound of weight in the next 12 months then you will have achieved your resolution. But is that what you really meant? Probably not!

The other thing that is missing here is strong emotion. You have got to know "why" you want to achieve these things. What is your real reason for losing weight? What will you do with the extra money that you make? How will these things make you feel?

So for example if you want to attract your ideal partner and you believe that having a slim and sexy body is the way to do this then think about how you will feel when you attract your ideal person? How strong are these feelings? You must have a strong reason or reasons for achieving any goal. If you don't then you are very unlikely to achieve anything.

Your goals have to excite you. The level of excitement needs to be so great that you actually experience pain if you do not follow through on them. So we are going to provide you with a method to set your goals that will make you so excited you will be bursting to get started on them!

By using this technique correctly then you will increase your confidence and self esteem. You will feel energized every time you read and think about your goals. When you set goals using this method it will help you to discover your strengths and weakness and you can work on these to achieve what you really want.

SMART FOR ME Goal Setting

So are you ready to write down your exciting and highly passionate goals? Good so get out some paper and a pen so that you can get started. If you keep a journal then record your goals in there. Don't use a computer or mobile device to do this. There is something about using a pen and paper to record your goals that is really empowering.

Once you have written your goals and you are excited about them then you can use a computer or mobile device to copy what you have written. But the initial goal setting must take place using a pen and paper. When you are writing your goals do not concern yourself with how you are going to achieve them. We will cover this later.

OK so let's explain the SMART FOR ME goal setting method. You may have heard about setting SMART goals before. This is an excellent technique that has been around for a long time and many people recommend it. We are going to use this and add some extra elements to it to ensure that your goals set you on fire!

Here is what the SMART goal setting process is all about:

Specific – you must set specific goals. What exactly do you want to achieve? Don't just say that you want to lose weight or earn extra money. Be specific about how much weight you want to lose (e.g. 30 pounds) or how much money you want to make (e.g. $100,000).

Measurable – it is essential that you can measure your goals so that you will know how well you are progressing. So with a weight loss goal you can step on the scales periodically to see how well you are doing. For earning more money keep a record of your income every month.

Attainable – this is all about totally believing that you can achieve the goal. We believe that you should go for whatever you want but if you are in your mid fifties and a bit overweight then being the next Olympic gold medal winner in most disciplines is not going to be attainable for you. Neither is making a million dollars over a weekend.

Realistic – is the goal you have set realistic? Do you have the resources, money and skills to achieve it? We are not asking you to limit yourself here but you must keep it real. You are not going to lose 30 pounds in a week nor are you going to learn to speak another language fluently in a short period of time.

Timed – there must be a deadline for each of your goals. This is pretty simple to understand. Choose a time frame to achieve your goal. Is it 3 months, 6 months or a year? These are all short periods of time.

OK now let's add the FOR component:

Focus – it is essential that you set focused goals. Don't commit to too many goals. We told you in the first chapter that 3 goals is probably the most that you can achieve at the same time. If this doesn't feel right then reduce this to 2 or even a single goal. Focusing on your goals is everything.

Optimism – you need to write your goals in a positive way so that they are optimistic. Negativity will kill your goals faster than you can believe. Do not use terms like "hope" and "wish" when writing your goals. Make it all positive.

Ready – you must be ready to start working on a goal right now. If you need to wait around for someone to assist you then your goal is not ready. All successful people always start right away. They get an idea and then spring into action immediately. They will make a call or write a plan or do some research. It doesn't matter what it is they just start.

And finally we have the ME component that will add true passion to your goals:

Meaningful – all of your goals need to tie in with your life's purpose. If you try to achieve a goal that doesn't gel with who you really are then you will struggle and probably not achieve it. Don't set goals that you know will conflict with your inner values.

Exciting – all goals that you set must be exciting. They must provide you with an emotional buzz to motivate you at the highest levels. So when you are writing your goals down think about how achieving them will make you feel. Make these feelings really intense and write them down.

In the next chapter we will talk about how you need to create a plan for the achievement of your goals...

Plan To Get
What You Want

Chapter 3

We told you in the first two chapters not to think about how you are going to achieve your goals. This is because getting bogged down with this kind of detail can start you thinking negatively and prevent you from actually going for the goal in the first place.

Look there are many ways that you can lose weight or make $100,000. Now is the time that you need to think about these things. You have probably heard the old saying:

"If you fail to plan then you are planning to fail".

This is very true. A goal without a plan is just a pipe dream. So you need to get your planning head on and start thinking about what you need to do each day to achieve your goals. It is not essential that your plan is perfect – in fact it is virtually impossible to come up with a perfect plan to achieve a challenging goal.

But you must start with a plan. As you progress you can make changes to it. The best plans are always reviewed regularly and changed to reflect reality. It is fine to have areas of your plan which are about research. In the beginning it is natural that you will need to find out more about how to do something.

Today we are lucky to have information at our fingertips on the Internet. Use this to your advantage. Whatever you want to achieve there will be someone who has done this already and shared their experiences online. So take a look at what they did and whether this is a good fit for you.

A Great Planning Technique

Do you remember that in the first chapter we asked you to take some quality time out with no distractions and ask yourself questions about your life so that you could figure out what you really want? Well we are going to ask you to do the same again to come up with a plan for your goals.

But there is a difference here. Instead of asking yourself a number of different questions we want you to ask yourself one question for each goal. You will then spend 20 to 30 minutes writing down the answers that come into your mind.

So if your goal is to earn $100,000 in the next 12 months then ask yourself a question like "how can I earn $100,000 in the next year?" Spend at least 20 minutes answering this question. If nothing is coming to mind then focus on the question again until it does.

Keep going with this until you really cannot come up with any more ideas. What you are doing here is asking your subconscious mind to come up with answers for you. Once you have a list for your plan you can add to it later. Before you go to sleep ask "subconscious mind please tell me how I can make $100,000 in a year".

If you have an idea in the middle of the night then have a pen and paper handy so that you can write it down and then go back to sleep. You may find that when you wake up in the morning you have more ideas – get them all down on paper. If the ideas sound crazy don't worry just write them down.

If one of your goals is to lose weight and you have failed at this before then your question could be "how can I lose 60 pounds in 12 months and not feel hungry" or "how can I lose 60 pounds in a year and not give in to temptations?"

A Plan with daily tasks

Once you have the ideas for your high level plan then the next step is to break this down into things that you can do each day to move you closer to your goal. When you take daily action towards your goal you make a statement to your subconscious mind that you are really serious about making this happen.

In turn your subconscious will do everything that it can to help you. If you were only to take action every few days then your subconscious would believe that you are not serious and provide no assistance to you at all. It is essential that you have your subconscious mind on your side at all times!

So for example one of your tasks for the first day could be to look at the different ways that you can make $100,000. This could be to get a higher paying job or even a second job. Or it could be to create a side hustle like an online business to make the additional money that you need.

For a weight loss goal you can research all of the different diet plans online to find one that will suit you. There are hundreds of these available. If you want to learn a new language then research the best way to do this in the shortest possible time.

Once you make a start on a daily plan you will find that new tasks emerge that you will need to complete the next day and so it goes on. The most important thing is to establish the tasks for the first day and then make a start straight away.

You must record your daily tasks. We recommend writing these down on paper or in a journal. If you want to use technology then that's fine. Just make sure that you can access your daily task list easily. A simple "to do" list can be really effective. Crossing off those things you have completed will motivate you and will help you to reflect on progress.

If you have something on your "to do" list that you were unable to complete then don't beat yourself up over this. Just transfer it to your task list for the next day and get it done then. When you do complete all of your daily tasks then give yourself a congratulatory pat on the back.

Accountability

If you work a job then you have a boss to be accountable to. If you are in a customer facing role then you are accountable to them as well. With a business it is all about being accountable to the customers. When you are working on your goals to achieve what you want in your life then you are accountable to nobody – unless you want to be.

Some people need others to be accountable to and others don't. If you are a true self starter then you probably do not need anyone. But if this is your first time setting goals and seriously trying to change your life for the better then it could be a good idea for you to have some accountability.

If you want someone to push you and motivate you then think about your circle of family and friends. Is there anyone in this group that will really tell you how it is and kick you in the rear if you are falling behind with your tasks? The last thing you want to do is to choose someone that will sympathize with you and say things like "never mind there is always tomorrow".

You need someone who will truly hold you accountable. If you are struggling to find someone then there are websites where you can declare your goals and the community will push you hard to achieve them.

Imagine this scenario. You are still working at your full time job and you have had a stressful day. You return home and there are your goal daily tasks waiting for you. So what do you do? Take the evening off? If you are not accountable to anyone then you can easily do this because only you will know that you have let yourself down.

If you have to explain your lack of activity to someone that you know will give you a hard time then this can be the extra push that you need to overcome the tiredness and tackle your tasks. You know which option is better don't you?

In the event that you cannot find a good "accountability partner" in your circle of family and friends and you don't really fancy the idea of sharing your dreams with strangers online then there is another option that you may find a little "out there". But bear with us because if you take this seriously it can really work well for you.

What we are talking about here is creating an "imaginary boss". This boss is going to hold you accountable and will praise you to the hilt when you do your daily tasks and stay on track and give you a verbal beating if you fall behind due to laziness.

If you adopt this idea then only you have to know about it. At the end of each day you will sit down with your imaginary boss and review what you have achieved. Your boss will pat you on the back if you have done well and kick you in the rear if you haven't. Give it a try for a while and take it seriously. It really works.

Don't Share your Goals with everyone

In some success books you will be encouraged to share your goals with everyone that you know. This is based on the premise that you will be accountable to many people and that it will spur you on to break through procrastination and keep on the right track with your daily plans.

But in our opinion this has a serious downside and we strongly recommend that you do not share your goals with everyone – just those that you can trust will use the information to encourage you.

Our reason for this is because without exception, everyone has negative people within their circle of family and friends. If you are currently earning $30,000 a year and so are most of your friends and you then suddenly announce that you will be earning $100,000 or more from the next year onwards then this will shock people and probably make them jealous.

They will find all kinds of ways to try and talk you out of this. You will hear things like "you will never do it" and "you haven't got what it takes". If you have mental toughness (which we will discuss in a later chapter) then you can just let these kinds of comments bounce off you and carry on regardless.

But if you are not at this point yet then this kind of negativity can be devastating to your progress. Sometimes people really close to you such as your parents or siblings may tell you that you are "wasting your time". Some may even laugh at you. So our advice is to keep everything to yourself until you have developed the mental toughness to deal with this.

In the next chapter we will discuss the need for you to control your thoughts to get what you really want…

Control
Your Thoughts
To Get What
You Want

Chapter 4

S o far we have discussed that to get what you want you need to:

- Identify what you really want

- Set exciting goals

- Create a plan to achieve your goals

Once you have done these 3 things you will be so far ahead of the vast majority of people! Now it is time for you to take action to achieve what you really want and this is by far the hardest thing to do.

Do you remember what we told you about taking action on a daily basis strengthening your subconscious mind? Not only that but your subconscious will see that you are serious and will help you to get what you want.

Use your Subconscious Mind to your advantage

You may not realize this but your subconscious mind is a all conquering tool that you need on your side to overcome the challenges that lay ahead. It will provide you with much needed intuition about how to tackle all of your problems.

Your thoughts are responsible for where you are today. Whatever you have or don't have in your life right now is down to your previous thoughts. So what do you think that you need to change to get what you really want?

That's right you need to change your thoughts

And it is not just about changing your thoughts either – you need to control them if you want success. Is this easy? No it isn't…

Is it possible? Yes it certainly is!

You have two minds which are your conscious and subconscious minds. Also within you are two opposing forces – we call these your higher and lower self. More on this in a bit.

Your subconscious mind is so powerful that it can provide you with everything that you need to get what you want.

But there is a downside. If you do not control your thoughts properly then your subconscious mind can make you give up. So how do you stop this? It is a simple matter of controlling what goes into your subconscious mind and what stays out.

You are in Control of your Thoughts

Always remember that you are in control of your thoughts. So if that is the case you can ensure that only the right things enter your subconscious mind. How do you do that? Well read on and we will tell you.

Before we get into thought control let's take a look at your two opposing forces that we call your "higher self" and your "lower self". These are best explained by way of examples:

Your Higher Self

This is the force within you that compels you to do the right things. You have a lot of tasks to complete in the pursuit of what you really want and your higher self provides the energy for you to tackle all of these tasks.

Your Lower Self

This is the force within you that looks for the path of least resistance. If you let your lower self dominate your life (as so many people do) then instead of getting on with your daily tasks you will sit on the couch and waste your life watching TV or spending hours on social media.

So how do you ensure that your higher self is uppermost and your lower self is kept well down (you can never completely get rid of this force)? The answer is that you need to control your thoughts.

How you can Control your Thoughts

Have you ever had a negative thought? Of course you have. We all have negative thoughts every day. These negative thoughts will totally destroy your dreams and will prevent you getting what you really want. So what can you do about this?

The answer is to neutralize your negative thoughts with positive ones. Yes it is that simple. The practice is a little more difficult of course. But the effort and persistence will pay off for you and you will be able to get what you want.

Negative people always end up with things that they don't want in their life. Positive people are far more likely to get what they want. So which one do you want to be? Most people are somewhere in the middle of being negative and positive. Use the techniques in this guide to swing over to the positive side.

The reason that negative people get things that they don't want is because of the Law of Attraction. This is a powerful life law that we will discuss in another chapter. For now just believe that positivity is the way to go if you want to get the things that you really want.

Getting rid of the Negativity in your life

If you really want to get what you want you are going to have to be more selfish. All of us have people in our family and friends circle that are negative. These people spend as much time as they can complaining about everything. It is always someone else's fault of course.

Each time that you are in the company of these people their negativity will have an impact on you. In the next chapter we are going to show you how you can develop the mental toughness needed to make sure that any negativity does not affect you and know you off course.

Until you get to that point you need a way to deal with the negativity of others. It is ridiculous for us to suggest that you never meet with these people ever again. Some of them will be loved family members and friends that you have had for years. But we do recommended that you cut down the amount of time that you spend with them.

When you are in their company and they start to question what you are doing then you need to handle this correctly if they make negative comments and criticisms. So if anyone says to you "you will never be able to do that" immediately neutralize this by thinking "I can do anything".

The other good way to deal with the negativity of others is to just treat what they say as their opinion. Everyone has opinions and some people love trying to force these on you. So when you hear something negative just think to yourself "this is just their opinion and they are not right".

Not all criticism is bad of course. If someone that you respect tries to give you constructive criticism about the way that you are doing something then always be prepared to listen. When you believe the criticism to be unjustified then just think "this is just their opinion and they are not right".

But if there is something valuable to you in the criticism then thank the person for pointing it out. As an example you may have decided to hire a mentor to help you get what you really want. This person has done what you are trying to do so you need to listen to what they tell you. It is your choice whether you accept their advice or not.

Another thing that we strongly recommend that you avoid is spending hours on social media. There are a ton of negative messages out there in the social space. You may think that you can handle it but in the beginning this can be really tough for you. We are not saying never use social media, but just cut down the time that you spend on it.

What about the news on TV? Some people just cannot miss the news and are happy to soak up all of the negativity that it brings. Our advice is to stop watching the news especially first thing in the morning. Don't start your day off with lots of negative messages surrounding you.

How to Control your own Thoughts

If you receive a negative comment from another person then you are less likely to believe this and internalize it than if it is a negative thought that just pops up in your head. This is because you trust yourself more than you do anyone else.

So if you suddenly think "I cannot do this" it is going to have much more of an impact than someone else telling you the same thing. What you need to do here is act on this negative thought immediately by thinking "I can do anything and I will figure this out" or something similar.

You do not want the negative thought "I can't do this" entering and embedding itself in your subconscious mind. If you don't neutralize thoughts like this then your subconscious will start believing that you can't do a lot of things which will have devastating consequences for you.

Did you ever wonder why some negative thoughts just seem to dominate you? This happens to everyone and the reason is that you are focusing on the problem rather than the solution. If you are having some financial problems and you don't have enough money for the rent then focusing on this problem will sap your energy and make you weak.

All of the time you will be thinking about not having the money to pay the rent. The answer to this is to focus on a solution. Ask yourself "what are the best ways for me to find the money to pay the rent?" Your subconscious will help you by providing some ideas.

When you do this you will free yourself from the negative spiral that you are in. You will have more energy to tackle the problem and come up with the right solution. So each time that you are up against it always focus on a solution rather than the problem.

Stop Living in the Past

Far too many people dwell in the past and let this rule their future. Just because you failed at something in the past doesn't mean that you will always fail at it in the future. We have all done this. There is something stopping us doing what we need to do and we let our past convince us that we will never overcome this problem.

This sends entirely the wrong messages to your subconscious mind. It strengthens the belief that you tried it once and failed and therefore you will always fail at it. Do you have a habit of giving up on new things easily? If you do this is because you have always done this. You are letting your past influence your future.

So how can you leave your past behind? Again it is all about controlling your thoughts. When you are going to start something new and a thought comes into your head like "I will not stick at this for long" then neutralize this immediately with something like "it doesn't matter that I gave up on things easily before, now I will see them through".

It is going to take persistent effort to make this work for you. There is no magic spell or overnight fix to control your thoughts. After a fairly short time of neutralizing your negative thoughts you will find that you have a much more positive outlook on life. This is the first sign that you are taking control of your thoughts.

Positive Affirmations

A lot of people laugh at the idea of using positive affirmations each day. But this is one of the best ways that you can make the transition from negative thinking to positive thinking. Even the most successful people have self doubts and think negatively about themselves. But in an instant they can snap out of this state and get back on the positive trail.

So what we recommend you do is spend some time thinking about your weaknesses. This may sound negative, but please bear with us here. Write down those weaknesses and then write a positive affirmation around each one of them.

If you believe that one of your weaknesses is to give up on new things too easily then you can create a positive affirmation that says "I never give up and always see things through until the end". Or maybe you are easily distracted so an affirmation could be "I am laser focused on getting what I want and I will not let any distractions get in my way".

Create your list of positive affirmations and then use them at least twice a day. Read them out loud when you get up and again before you go to sleep at night. Over time this will make a massive impact on your positivity and you will develop the power to do anything that you want.

In the next chapter we will discuss how you can develop mental toughness that will help you to get what you really want...

Developing
The Mental Toughness
To Get What You Want

Chapter 5

If you really want to get what you want then you have to ensure that you never give up. There are going to be times when you are faced with problems that you don't know how to solve and this can overwhelm you. Then there will be times when you are tired and do not have the energy to get your tasks done.

Everyone has these problems so how do the elite few overcome these issues and keep moving forward? The answer is that they have a mental toughness that sees them through the tough times. They have what we call an "iron resolve" which means that whatever situation they are in they will get through it and keep going.

Successful people that have this mental toughness do not waste their time on meaningless things like watching hours of TV and social media. If they are overwhelmed by something they quickly snap out of this state and then keep on going. They never let their lower self dominate their life.

Use the Law of Inertia

What is the Law of Inertia? The best way to explain it is that it is difficult to change at the beginning but once you have worked on that change for a while there will be a great force to keep going with it.

You need to constantly battle with your lower self that is telling you to give up and sit on the couch. This leads to lethargy and procrastination. Using the Law of Inertia you can strengthen your higher self so that it becomes dominant and keeps you on track.

In order to do this you have to push yourself to do something even when you do not feel like doing it. You are going to have bad days where you just don't want to work on your tasks. The best way to get out of this state is to push through it. When you do this you will confirm to your subconscious mind that you are a real action taker.

Traits for Mental Toughness

So just how do you develop the mental toughness necessary to ward off negativity and keep going whatever is happening around you? Well you need to develop six traits that will make you more mentally strong and provide you with an iron resolve. Here are the 6 traits you need for mental toughness:

1. Start

2. Prioritize

3. Focus

4. Persistence

5. Review

6. Organization

Let's take a look at each of these in turn.

Start

If you want to get what you want then you have to "start". And that means start right now! Don't wait around for anyone or anything. The time to start is right now! When you start you will utilize the power of inertia. Writing a book starts with the first few words. SO just make a start and keep going.

But what if you can't make a start right now? What if the thing that you want to do is just too difficult for you? Never believe that anything is too difficult for you. Just make a start on it. Most things are nowhere near as difficult as they seem at first. Break a large task down into smaller components and make a start.

If you have too many things on your daily "to do" list and don't know where to start then this can overwhelm you and it can lead you to starting nothing. So in this situation you need to develop the second trait which is to…

Prioritize

OK so you have 7 tasks that you want to complete today. Which one do you start with? We recommend that you start with that task that will nag at you all day if you don't do it. Maybe this is paying a bill or responding to an important email. For some reason you have been putting this off and now the pressure is really on.

You do not want to have this kind of pressure in your life so just do this thing first. You will feel so much better afterwards and empowered to get the other tasks done. If something is stressing you out then it will be hard to concentrate on your other tasks.

The next priority is to choose the easiest task on your list. Maybe you have always been told to tackle the most difficult thing first but we do not agree with this. By tackling something easy you build momentum to move on and use the Law of Inertia to your advantage.

This does not mean that you should procrastinate over difficult tasks of course. They need to get done as well. It's just a lot easier to tackle the more difficult tasks when you have the momentum from already completing a task and you are not stressed.

So after a task that is going to stress you out if you don't complete it and completing the easiest task on your list for momentum you need to take a look at the remaining tasks and prioritize them in order of importance. The do each one in order.

Focus

The ability to concentrate fully on what you are doing until it is complete is one of the most powerful tools for your mental toughness. It is tougher now to focus on things than it ever was before because today's world is full of distractions.

Make sure that you avoid obvious distractions. Don't try to work on your tasks with the TV blaring in the background. Similarly it will be really tough for you to complete your tasks in a room full of people that are talking. You know the things that are going to distract you so avoid them.

It is almost impossible not to be distracted all of the time. When this happens you need to refocus on what you were doing again. If you are the type of person that has a wandering mind then keep refocusing until it becomes second nature.

Persistence

This is another great mental toughness trait that you simply must develop. Persistence wins wars, wins gold medals at the Olympics, creates multibillion dollar companies and finds cures for diseases. It is the total opposite of giving up.

When you give up on something, no matter how small, you let your lower self creep back into your life. Your subconscious receives the wrong signals and this will make you more likely to give up again in the future.

Why do people give up on stuff? One of the most common reasons is fear of failure. Do you think that people that have everything in their life didn't make mistakes and feel like giving up at some point? Of course not. But they didn't give up because they were persistent. They learned from their failures and they moved forward.

If you are in a situation where you feel like giving up then get out your goal sheet and read the reasons why you are doing this. This will light a fire under you and give you the motivation to keep on going.

Stand up and move your body. Punch the air and say out loud "come on" to give yourself renewed energy.

Keep working on your persistence. It is a very valuable mental toughness trait to have. You will never get what you really want if you keep giving up. Persistent people always win the day.

Review

This one may have you a little puzzled. Why is this necessary for mental toughness? It is very important to review what you are doing regularly to see if you are on the right track. If you don't do this then you can spend a lot of time and energy moving in the wrong direction.

Let's say that one of your goals is to lose weight. One way to review this is to step on the scales regularly. But there is more to it than that. Does your new regime make you hungry and tired? Are you feeling healthier through what you are doing or more unhealthy?

When you review the things that you are doing it will tell you what is working and what isn't. You can do more of what is working and take a different approach with the things that are not working out as you expected. So plan regular reviews of your progress towards your goals. You really need to know if you are on the right path or not.

Organization

If you are disorganized in your life then this will present you with a number of challenges that you can easily avoid. Imagine needing something to complete a task and not having a clue where it is. This can be a computer file or a physical document for example. You have to find it and this will stress you out and waste your valuable time.

There is no magic wand to wave for better organization. It is just something that you have to do. When you receive or create a new computer file save it in a place where you know you can easily find it in the future. Don't just save it anywhere. Over time you can build up thousands or even millions of files on your computer.

A simple folder system will work. Each time you work on something new create a new folder for it. It will only take a few seconds to do this and will save you a ton of time in the future when you need to refer back to the important files that you have.

Organize all of your important papers as well. Use a small filing cabinet or home organizer so that you can easily locate things. Turning your home upside down to find a document is very frustrating and will put you in a bad mood.

In the next chapter we will discuss how to use the Law of Attraction to get what you want...

Using The Law
Of Attraction To
Get What You
Want

Chapter 6

I n this chapter we will explain how you can use the power of the Law of Attraction to get what you really want. We will tell you what the Law of Attraction is and what it isn't and provide you with some powerful methods to really make it work for you.

The Law of Attraction explained

So what is the Law of Attraction? It is a universal law that works on the principle that like attracts like. Everything in the Universe vibrates including human beings. This vibration is not visible to the naked eye but it does exist. Everything communicates with the Universe through this vibration.

It is a really good thing that you cannot see everything vibrating because it would probably drive you crazy. Humans emit their vibrations to the Universe through their thoughts and feelings.

If you transmit negative thoughts and feelings to the Universe then you will get negativity in return. On the other hand if your thoughts and feelings are positive then the Universe will help you to manifest the things that you really want in your life.

So the way to use the Law of Attraction to get what you really want is to send high energy, positive thoughts and feelings to the Universe. Everything that we have covered so far in this guide will enable you to do that.

What the Law of Attraction is not

The Law of Attraction is not some magic spell. You may have heard that some people just wish for something good to happen in their lives and the Law of Attraction manifests this for them. The movie The Secret certainly suggests this.

You certainly need to focus on what you want to get it but it takes more than thought. When you have clarity of thought and focus the Universe will open certain doors for you to be able to manifest your desires. But that is not the end of the story.

Taking action is the other part of the story. Some people say they have used the Law of Attraction to win the lottery. Whether this is true or not is hard to tell but in order to win the lottery these people needed to take action. They had to purchase lottery tickets and choose the numbers that they wanted to play.

When you are working on your plan for your goal you will send the right signals to the Universe. This will strengthen your connection and will help the Universe to manifest what you really want. Sitting on the couch thinking and hoping will never achieve anything.

There are three additional things that you can do as well as what you have learned so far to harness the power of the Law of Attraction:

Ask the Universe for what you really want

Ask and you will receive. This is an old saying that is very true. The Universe will manifest what you really want if you ask for it and then maintain positive vibrations and high levels of energy to get it. These positive vibrations will come from the work that you do each day to achieve your goal.

We recommend that you create a statement to the Universe and read this out loud every day. Here is an example:

I am very grateful to the Universe because by 31 December 2020 I will have $500,000 in my possession, and this will be an easy sum of money for me to earn. I will earn this money by providing a lot of value to people on the Internet. I will teach them how to be successful online. The more people that I am able to help, the more money I will earn. I see myself with the money in my hands, I can see all of the money with my eyes, I can smell the money with my nose. I have total belief that I possess $500,000 and I am extremely grateful. Thank you Universe. Thank you Universe.

Be sure to write your Universe statement down on paper and carry it around with you at all times. Read it out loud when you get up and before you go to bed (like you do with your positive affirmations).

Imagine that you already have what you really want

You will send out very strong vibrations to the Universe if you imagine that you already have what you want in your life. One of the best ways to do this is to use visualization. Here you will see yourself with the thing that you really want. You need to add strong emotion here by imagining how you will feel when you have what you want.

It is not that difficult to visualize. Some people find it really easy to do while others take a bit of time to master it. It is a very powerful tool so keep at it until you can visualize on autopilot.

Believe in the Law of Attraction and that you will get what you really want

You need unshakeable belief in the Law of Attraction and total belief that you will achieve your goals and get what you really want. This means that your belief will not waver if anyone tries to talk you out of it or you read something that says it is all nonsense.

There is no miracle fix here. You just need to strengthen your belief in the Law of Attraction and your goals every day. Reading your Universe statement and reflecting on your goals every day will help to do this. Developing your mental toughness is also going to help you.

In the next chapter we will discuss how you can be raise your confidence levels to get what you really want...

Raise Your
Confidence Levels
To GetWhat You
Really Want

Chapter 7

On your journey towards getting what you really want you are going to need confidence. Confidence in your ability to do something, confidence to approach people that can help you and so on. A lot of people do not have this kind of confidence and think that it is a gift that only some people possess.

This is nonsense.

You can increase your confidence any time that you want. With the methods in this chapter you will have the confidence to give a public speech rather than run a mile. You will have the confidence to tackle problems that you have never experienced in the past. In fact you will have the confidence to do anything…

Tackling your Fears

Fear is the reason that people are not confident. They do not want to approach an attractive girl or boy because they fear rejection. They do not want to try new things because they have a fear of failure and that people will laugh at them. Does any of this sound familiar?

This is irrational fear and every time you accept it you will strengthen it and your lower self will come to the surface and tell you that you don't need to do this thing. Everyone has irrational fears and the best way to deal with them is to tackle them head on.

So if you need to do something new to achieve your goal then just tell yourself that you can do it and then do it! If you fail the first time it doesn't matter. Just get back on your horse and try again! After facing your fears head on for a while you will find that you will easily be able to do the things you always dreaded.

You are expanding your comfort zone and sending strong signals to your subconscious mind and to the Universe. Facing your fears head on is the best way to overcome them. It is going to be tough at first but in a short time you will overcome them completely.

Develop your Self Respect

We want you to be so confident that you can do anything. In order to get to this level you will need to strengthen your self respect. If you have a low opinion of yourself then you have a bit of work to do. But in no time at all you can have very high self esteem.

Think about things that you have achieved in the past. Maybe you learned to drive or passed some tough exams. It doesn't really matter what it was as long as it was challenging for you. Once you had achieved these things how did you feel?

Did you have a strong feeling of satisfaction? Were you really proud of yourself? Recreate these feelings and make the strong. You can use these feelings to generate the confidence that you need in a snap to tackle anything in your life.

Create a Physical Anchor

If you want to have super confidence at any time then you can create a physical anchor. This is really easy to do and will help you when you need a confidence boost. In the last section we asked you to recall something challenging that you did and then experience the strong feelings that resulted from this.

Now it is time to use this to your advantage. Recall a past event where you overcame the odds and were successful. Experience the strong feelings of pride and satisfaction. At the same time squeeze your thumb and forefinger together to create a physical anchor.

So the next time that you need a confidence boost all you need to do is to squeeze your thumb and forefinger together in the same way and you will experience those strong feelings again. This really works. The secret is to make the feelings as strong as possible when you are creating the anchor.

If you do not experience the strong feelings when you use this physical anchor then repeat the anchoring process again. The feelings were not strong enough when you did it the first time around. Once you have this anchor in place you can use it anytime and anywhere for a great confidence boost.

In the next chapter we will talk about your daily routine for getting what you really want...

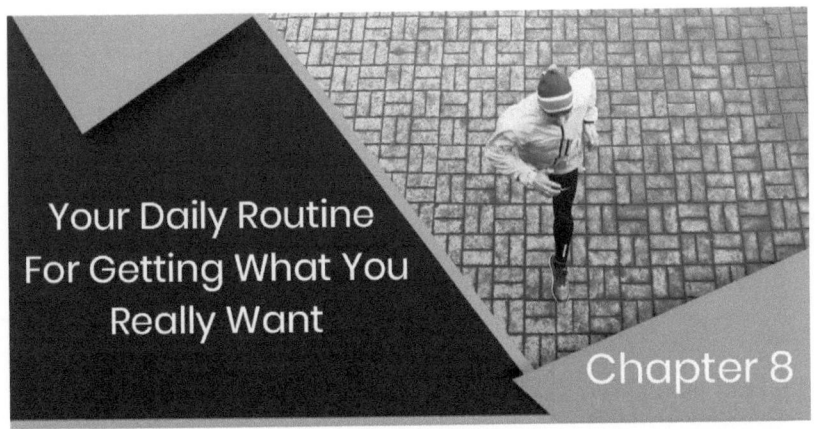

Your Daily Routine For Getting What You Really Want

Chapter 8

I f you want to get what you really want then you need to establish a daily routine to support this. This involves taking consistent action each day and sending the strongest signals to your subconscious mind and the Universe that you really want the thing you desire.

Start the Day off right

Getting a good start to the day is essential. You want to make a positive start rather than a negative one. So here is what we recommend you do:

- Read your goal statement and your reasons for wanting to achieve the goal(s)

- Read your statement to the Universe
- Read your positive affirmations
- Visualize that you already have what you really want
- Plan your day and start working on one task

All of these things will help to send the right signals to your subconscious mind and the Universe. They will also help to develop your mental toughness (especially persistence) and strengthen your belief that you will get what you desire.

Use a Journal

If you don't have a journal then we highly recommend that you start to use one right now. You can record your goals in the journal as well as your statement to the Universe and your positive affirmations. It is also a good idea to record your daily tasks in your journal.

Make a note of your feelings as you continue your journey. Each day make an entry in your journal about what you have done and how you feel. Note any obstacles that you had to overcome.

After you have made a few journal entries you can reflect back on how far you have come. This is great for extra motivation. If you are feeling down for any reason then get out your journal and recall what you have achieved so far.

Learn something New each day

Be committed to life learning. Learning does not end when you leave school. This is just the beginning. Make a commitment to learn at least one new thing each day. It doesn't matter how small this is. Keep building on your knowledge all of the time.

End the Day right

Before you retire at night we recommend that you do the following:

- Read your goal statement and your reasons for wanting to achieve the goal(s)
- Read your statement to the Universe
- Read your positive affirmations
- Visualize that you already have what you really want
- Plan for the next day

Again you are sending the strongest signals to your subconscious mind and the Universe. You will sleep soundly knowing that you have planned out the next day.

Handling Inactivity

There are going to be times when you just cannot complete your daily actions, or even start them because something happens in your life to prevent this. This could be a tragedy like a death in the family or some other kind of emergency.

Whenever you miss a day for whatever reason don't beat yourself up over it. During the same day find a few minutes on your own when you can think about your actions and your goals. Do this in the bathroom if you have to!

Carry a piece of paper and a pen with you and then write a mini plan on how you will recover from this inactivity. You may need to re-prioritize the actions so that the next day you tackle the really important ones first.

The important thing is that you think about your goal and your actions. You need to keep telling your subconscious mind and the Universe that you are serious and really want to manifest your desires.

This really works and will only take a few minutes. We are realistic and understand that these things happen.

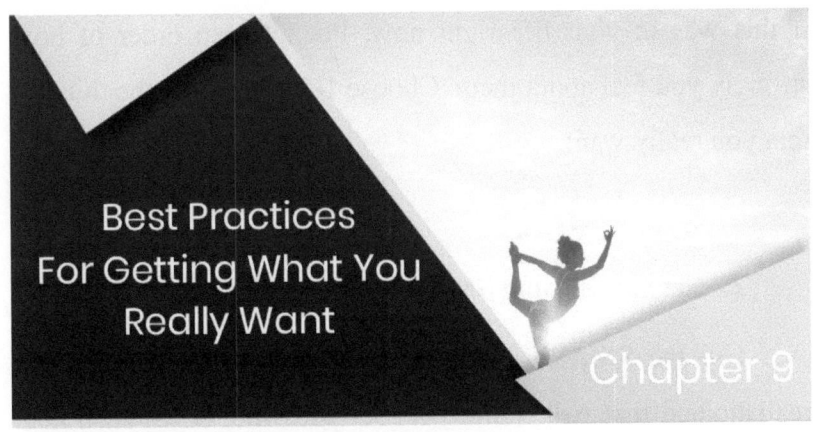

Best Practices For Getting What You Really Want

Chapter 9

Here are the best practices that we highly recommend that you follow to get what you really want. We want you to succeed and by following these 8 best practices you will give yourself the maximum chance of getting everything that you want in your life.

1. Determine what you Really want

Take the time out to think about different aspects of your life. Use the questions in chapter one and write down your answers. Reflect on each answer and imagine how you will feel if this was in your life right now. Put these in order of how strongly you feel about them. Choose 1-3 of these as the thing(s) that you really want.

2. Set Goals using SMART FOR ME

Use the SMART FOR ME process to set goals that are realistic and that will excite you. As you write down each goal on paper add the real reason why you want to achieve the goal. Be careful not to take on too many goals. We recommend that 3 is a maximum.

3. Create a Plan to achieve your Goal

Spend time creating a plan to achieve your goal(s). You will use this plan to create daily, weekly and monthly tasks. Having daily tasks is very important as when you work on these tasks you will send the right signals to your subconscious mind and the Universe.

4. Control your Thoughts

Controlling your thoughts is crucial to get what you really want. If you live in a world of negativity then your subconscious mind will never believe that you are serious. Neutralize all negative thoughts with positive ones. Stop dwelling in the past and avoid negativity as much as you can. Create and use positive affirmations.

5. Develop Mental Toughness

Mental toughness will help you to overcome any barriers and brush off negativity so that you can keep working towards what you really want. You need to develop the following 6 traits:

1. Start

2. Prioritize

3. Focus

4. Persistence

5. Review

6. Organization

6. Harness the Power of the Law of Attraction

Use the power of the Law of Attraction to get what you really want. Write a statement to the Universe and read this each day. Reflect on your goals every day and do your daily actions to send the right signals to the Universe. Visualize that you already have what you want and experience how good this feels. Believe that it will work for you.

7. Increase your Confidence

You will need to be as confident as possible to achieve your goals and get what you really want. Face your fears head on and do it anyway. Develop your self respect by reflecting on past achievements. Create a physical anchor so that you can increase your confidence at any time.

8. Develop a Daily Routine

Start the day off right by reflecting on your goal(s), reading your statement to the Universe, reading your positive affirmations and planning your tasks and work on at least one task. Start a journal and make an entry each day. At the end of each day reflect on your goal(s), read your statement to the Universe, read your positive affirmations and plan your tasks for the next day.

Conclusion

Y ou now know everything that you need to do to get what you really want. It is now your turn to take action and make it happen. Don't just read this guide and then let it gather digital dust on your hard drive. This is your life so follow the steps and apply what you have learned.

Most people have no idea what they really want so by deciding this you will be streets ahead of the majority of the population. But don't stop there – set your goals and take the actions necessary to achieve them.

Work tirelessly on controlling your thoughts and developing the mental toughness you need to keep on going when things get difficult. And you need to believe that things will get difficult for you.

We hope that you enjoyed reading "Get What You Really Want" and that you found this guide informative and inspiring. Start right now by identifying what you really want and then follow through with the rest of the advice and guidance provided here. We sincerely hope that you get what you want in your life.

Printed by Libri Plureos GmbH in Hamburg,
Germany